Adventure Guide to Maine's Down East Sunrise Trail

Please Help Keep Our Trails Open

Please stay on all marked trails and respect signs you see posted. Road closures are often temporary and for the safety of all, but will become permanent if temporary closures are not respected.

Stay Safe

Stay on the right side of all trails, especially around corners.
Stay on marked trails to avoid putting yourself and your group in danger.
Don't drink and ride. Maine has a tough OUI law.
Yield for logging operations and equipment.
Don't chase moose or other wildlife. If provoked they may attack you.

Using this publication means you hold the publisher, ATV clubs, snowmobile clubs, property owners, and any other parties who contributed to the creation of this publication harmless for any physical injury or property damage sustained through the use of this publication or these trails. The publisher and all contributors accept absolutely no responsibility for the trails being opened or closed, nor the condition of the trails.

ALWAYS CONTACT LOCAL ATV & SNOWMOBILE CLUBS FOR THE MOST CURRENT TRAIL CLOSURES AND INFORMATION.

Please Note: Outdoor adventure and exploration is potentially hazardous. The publisher and author did their best to ensure accuracy of all information at the time of publication, however, they cannot accept responsibility for any loss, injury, or inconvenience experienced by anyone as a result of information or advice in this book. Also, land ownership and trails change over time. If you discover changes in ownership, trails, or any other inaccurate information please let us know so we can correct it for future editions. The author and publisher also welcome any comments or suggestions.

Contact us at:
Untamed Mainer
PO Box 109
Little Deer Isle, ME 04650
Ang@UntamedMainer.com

Over 90% of Maine's ATV, Dirt Bike, & Snowmobile Trails are on Private Land.

Please help us keep them open.

Stay on marked trails. Only trails marked specifically for ATVs, Dirt Bikes, & Snowmobiles are legal trails.

Respect trail closures. Trails can be closed completely, temporarily, or only to dirt bikes. Contact local clubs for the most updated trail information. Please respect the landowners request to close trails or we may lose access to other trails.

If you see trailside garbage or items left by others, please pick them up. Landowners won't allow public access to their lands if they're being trashed.

All of Maine's ATV, Dirt Bike & Snowmobile Trails are Maintained by Volunteers.

Please join a local club and volunteer your time to help improve the trails and make them last for years to come!

Local clubs and their contact information can be found on the map pages and on page 8 & 9. Many clubs also have a Facebook page you can use to contact them for updated trail information.

CONTENTS

LEGEND

ATV ONLY TRAILS

SNOWMOBILE ONLY TRAILS

ATV & SNOWMOBILE TRAILS

DOWN EAST SUNRISE TRAIL

PAVED ACCESS ROUTES

 PARKING LOCATION

 FUEL

 CLUBHOUSE

 PICNIC TABLE

 OUTHOUSE

 CAMPSITE

 CAMPGROUND

 NATURAL LANDMARK

DEST PERMITTED USES

DOWN EAST SUNRISE TRAIL
MULTI-USE TRAIL SYSTEM

TRAIL SYSTEM MADE POSSIBLE BY MAINE DEPT. OF CONSERVATION, MAINEDOT, COOPERATING PRIVATE LANDOWNERS, NATIONAL-RECREATION TRAILS ACT (FEDERAL HIGHWAY ADMINISTRATION), AND THE MAINE STATE LEGISLATURE

PERMITTED USES

SUMMER

USER ETHICS WHEN MEETING ON TRAIL
PLEASE YIELD TO THOSE
PASSING FROM BEHIND
PASS ON LEFT WITH CAUTION

WINTER

THE DOWN EAST SUNRISE TRAIL (DEST) IS OPEN 24/7

MOTORIZED SUMMER PERMITTED USES:
ATVs, dirt bikes, Dual Sport motorcycles, scooters/mopeds
All motorized vehicles must be legally registered as an ATV in the state of Maine to be on the DEST. Registrations must be renewed every year by June 30th.

NON-MOTIRIZED SUMMER PERMITTED USES INCLUDE BUT ARE NOT LIMITED TO:
Walking, hiking, horseback riding, bicycling

MOTORIZED WINTER PERMITTED USES:
Snowmobiles
All snowmobiles must be legally registered in the state of Maine to be on the DEST. Registrations must be renewed every year by June 30th.

NON-MOTIRIZED WINTER PERMITTED USES
INCLUDE BUT ARE NOT LIMITED TO:
Snowshoeing, skiing, fat biking, dog sledding

GENERAL INFORMATION

TRAIL CLOSINGS

CONSTRUCTION AND MUD SEASON CLOSINGS:

Sometimes sections of the trail will become washed out or need repairs. If construction is required on a section of the trail, a sign reading "CONSTRUCTION ZONE, NO TRESPASSING" will be posted and that section of the trail will be *closed to all public use, including pedestrian traffic.*

Trails are closed during mud season and signs will be posted reading "STOP! TRAIL TEMPORARILY CLOSED DUE TO SATURATED SOILS" although *pedestrian traffic is permitted during mud season which includes walking, jogging, or hiking only.*

WINTER CLOSINGS:

Snow conditions on the trail determine what the trail can be used for. **If snow is on the trail ATVs and horseback riding is not permitted.**

Permitted uses when snow is covering the trail include snowmobiling, skiing, snowshoeing, dog sledding, bicycling, and hiking.

If the trail is not snow-covered but is frozen and conditions are ideal, ATV and horseback riding are permitted unless the trail has been officially closed for the season.

YIELD TO HORSES

HOW TO PASS HORSES & RIDERS SAFELY

All users of the DEST must yield to horses. Horses can be unpredictable, and the key to passing safely is communication with the rider. The last thing anyone wants is a 900+ pound animal freaking out on the trail- it can be dangerous for everyone involved.

No matter what mode of transportation you're using, you should:

1. Pull-over to the side of the trail when you see a horse approaching.
2. If you're on a motorized vehicle, shut off the machine, and take off your helmet.
3. Say "hi" to the rider so the horse knows you're a human and not a threat.
4. Ask the rider what they would like you to do if they don't give you instructions.
5. Let the horse and rider gain some distance from you before restarting your engine or taking off.
6. Take off slowly until you get some more distance between you and the horse.

When approaching a horse and rider from behind, go very slowly and wait for the rider to realize you're there. Wait for the rider to give you instructions on how to pass them, and if they don't, ask them what to do. Some riders may motion you to pass if they have a horse used to off-road machines. Others may need to pull off to the side of the trail, and some may need to dismount and hold their horse while you pass slowly on the opposite side of the trail.

HORSEBACK RIDING ON THE DEST

Horseback riders should let other trail users know how to pass them. Stay alert and pull off the trail when you hear motorized riders approaching. Remember, they won't know you're there until they see you. When riding in a group, always put the steadiest most confident horse in the lead.

GENERAL INFORMATION

DOGS & HORSES ON THE DEST

BRING WATER!

While there are many ponds, streams, rivers, and marshes along the DEST, it isn't always easy (or possible) to get to water along the trail. There are many places where the rail bed is built up rather steep next to water bodies making it dangerous to try and get to the water. Bring water and something to put it in like a collapsible bowl for your dog or horse.

BRING A LEASH

Dogs on the DEST must be leashed. Other trail users, especially motorized vehicles, may not see you when coming around a corner, and a loose dog can be extremely dangerous, especially if it runs out in front of another trail user.

CAMPING ON THE DEST

FIRE PERMITS

There are several different places to go camping on the DEST, or located not far from the DEST, that may or may not require a fire permit.

Campsites in the Donnell Pond Public Lands do not require a fire permit with the exception of the two campsites located on Spring River Lake, which is north of Route 182.

Sunrise Campground, the trailside campground located on Cherryfield Stretch, does not require fire permits, although fires can only be built in the provided fire rings.

SUNRISE CAMPGROUND

Sunrise Campground is located between Cherryfield and Harrington on the DEST. This is a free campground that has six tent sites. Campfires are only permitted where a fire ring is present. Each site also has a picnic table, and a porta-potty is located at the entrance of the campground.

For additional questions about fire permits contact:
Maine Forest Protection, Central Region Headquarters
87 Airport Rd, Old Town: (207) 827-1800

Bridge in Cherryfield

Sunrise Campground in Milbridge

DEST ATV Clubs

Listed Alphabetical by Town Name, Number Indicates Marker Number on Map
Clubs without numbers are outside of the DEST and are included for those taking trips beyond the DEST

Alexander- Breakneck Mountain ATV Club
https://www.facebook.com/BreakneckMountainATV/
PO Box 1384, Calais, ME 04619

Llewellyn Dwelley, Jr., President
beberhart@peoplepc.com
207-454-3747
Steven Parks, Trail Master
skparks80@gmail.com
207-214-5830

Beddington- Airline Swamp Donkey ATV Club
https://www.emainehosting.com/AirlineATVers/
154 Lakeview Lane, Crawford, ME 04694

Frank Janusz- President
207-454-8133
David Bridges & Peter Poors- Trail Masters
207-460-4474

128   Calais- Sunrise Trail Riders
https://www.facebook.com/groups/246184952537394/
11 Church Street, Calais, ME 04619

Bill Lee, President
207-214-8740

116 Cherryfield- Narraguagus ATV Club
https://www.facebook.com/NarraguagusAtvClub/
narraguagusatv@earthlink.net
207-546-2730
PO Box 453, Cherryfield, ME 04622

Mary Young, President
marylouiseknapp1@yahoo.com
207-598-8188
Ray Young, Trail Master
207-598-8184

Cutler- East Stream ATV Riders
http://www.oocities.org/esatvc02/index.html
PO Box 361, Cutler, ME 04626

Matt Kalloch, President
mkalloch@verison.net
207-259-3832
Sterling Fitzhenry, Trail Master
cfitz1918@live.com
207-259-0988

111 Dennysville- Dennysville Snowmobile & ATV Club
Clubhouse is open 24/7 and has a vending machine and tables inside
https://www.facebook.com/Dennysville-Snowmobile-ATV-Club-211484195
580103/
207-263-6306
PO Box 45, 24 Milwaukee Road, Dennysville, ME 04628

112 East Machias- Down East Trailriders
https://www.facebook.com/detrail.riders?ref=br_rs
PO Box 658, East Machias, ME 04630

Grant Hanscom, President
ghanscom@roadrunner.com
207-557-7816
Scott Ackley, Trail Master
207-263-5880

Eddington- Airline ATV Riders
http://emainehosting.com/AirlineATVRiders/
PO Box 14, Eddington, ME 04428

Earl Oak, President
eoak2@roadrunner.com
207-843-7351
Moe Schinck, Trail Master
207-299-4009

48   Ellsworth- Acadia Area ATV'ers
https://www.acadiaareaatvers.com/
PO Box 1676, Ellsworth, ME 04605
Clubhouse: Washington Junction Road, Hancock, ME 04640

Edward Jellison, President
ejellison@yahoo.com
207-460-6825
Walter Bell, Trail Master
207-963-2506

Grand Lake Stream- Grand Lake Stream ATV Club
http://www.glsatvclub.com/
15 Water Street Unit #2, Grand Lake Stream, ME 04668

Deanna Sainati, President
847-609-6687
Al LaPlante, Trail Master
allaplante1@gmail.com
207-796-5050

117 Machias- Ridge Riders Trail Club
PO Box 200, Machias, ME 04654
rrtrailclub@yahoo.com

118 Robbinston- Robbinston Bushwackers
PO Box 45, Robbinston, ME 04671

Kevin Murray, President
kmurray922@hotmail.com
207-214-5253
Brent Lyons, Trail Master
blyons28@yahoo.com
207-214-6297
Robbie Lyons, Trail Master
robbie_lyons@hotmail.com
207-214-7293

DEST Snowmobile Clubs

Listed Alphabetical by Town Name, Number Indicates Marker Number on Map

Clubs without numbers are outside of the DEST and are included for those taking trips beyond the DEST

Alexander- Breakneck Mountain Sno-Riders
https://www.facebook.com/pages/category/Community/Breakneck-Mountain-Sno-riders-180921661932368/
PO Box 1384, Calais, ME 04619

Llewellyn Dwelley, Jr., President
beberhart@peoplepc.com
207-454-3747
Steven Parks, Trail Master
skparks80@gmail.com
207-214-5830

Beddington- Airline Riders Snowmobile Club
https://www.emainehosting.com/AirlineRiders/
154 Lakeview Lane, Crawford, ME 04694

Frank Janusz- President
207-454-8133
David Bridges & Peter Poors- Trail Masters
Pete 207-460-4474
Frank 207-454-8133
Mayrann 207-546-1178

128   Calais- Sunrise Snowmobilers
https://www.facebook.com/SunriseSnowmobilers
11 Church Street, Calais, ME 04619

Bill Lee, President
207-214-8740
sunrisesnowmobilers@gmail.com

116 Cherryfield- Narraguagus Snowmobile Club
https://www.facebook.com/NarraguagusSnowmobile
207-546-7205
334 Ridge Road, Cherryfield, ME 04622
Narr.SC@gmail.com

111 Dennysville- Dennysville Snowmobile & ATV Club
Clubhouse is open 24/7 and has a vending machine and tables inside
https://www.facebook.com/Dennysville-Snowmobile-ATV-Club-211484195580103/
207-263-6306
PO Box 45, 24 Milwaukee Road, Dennysville, ME 04628

112 East Machias- Down East Trailriders
https://www.facebook.com/detrail.riders?ref=br_rs
PO Box 658, East Machias, ME 04630

Grant Hanscom, President
ghanscom@roadrunner.com
207-557-7816
Scott Ackley, Trail Master
207-263-5880

48   Ellsworth- Ellsworth Snowmobile Club
https://www.facebook.com/Ellsworth-Snowmobile-Club-261762404825428/
ellsworthsnowmobileclub@gmail.com

Grand Lake Stream- Grand Lake Snowmobile Club
http://www.grandlakesnowmobileclub.com/
1 Webber Dirt Road, Grand Lake Stream, ME 04668
grandlakesnowmobileclub@gmail.com

Trail Master- Les @ Pine Tree Store 207-796-5027

117 Machias- Ridge Riders Trail Club
PO Box 200, Machias, ME 04654
rrtrailclub@yahoo.com
https://www.facebook.com/groups/443675609142367/

Washington Junction
parking lot, clubhouse,
and trailhead in Hancock,
mile marker 2.

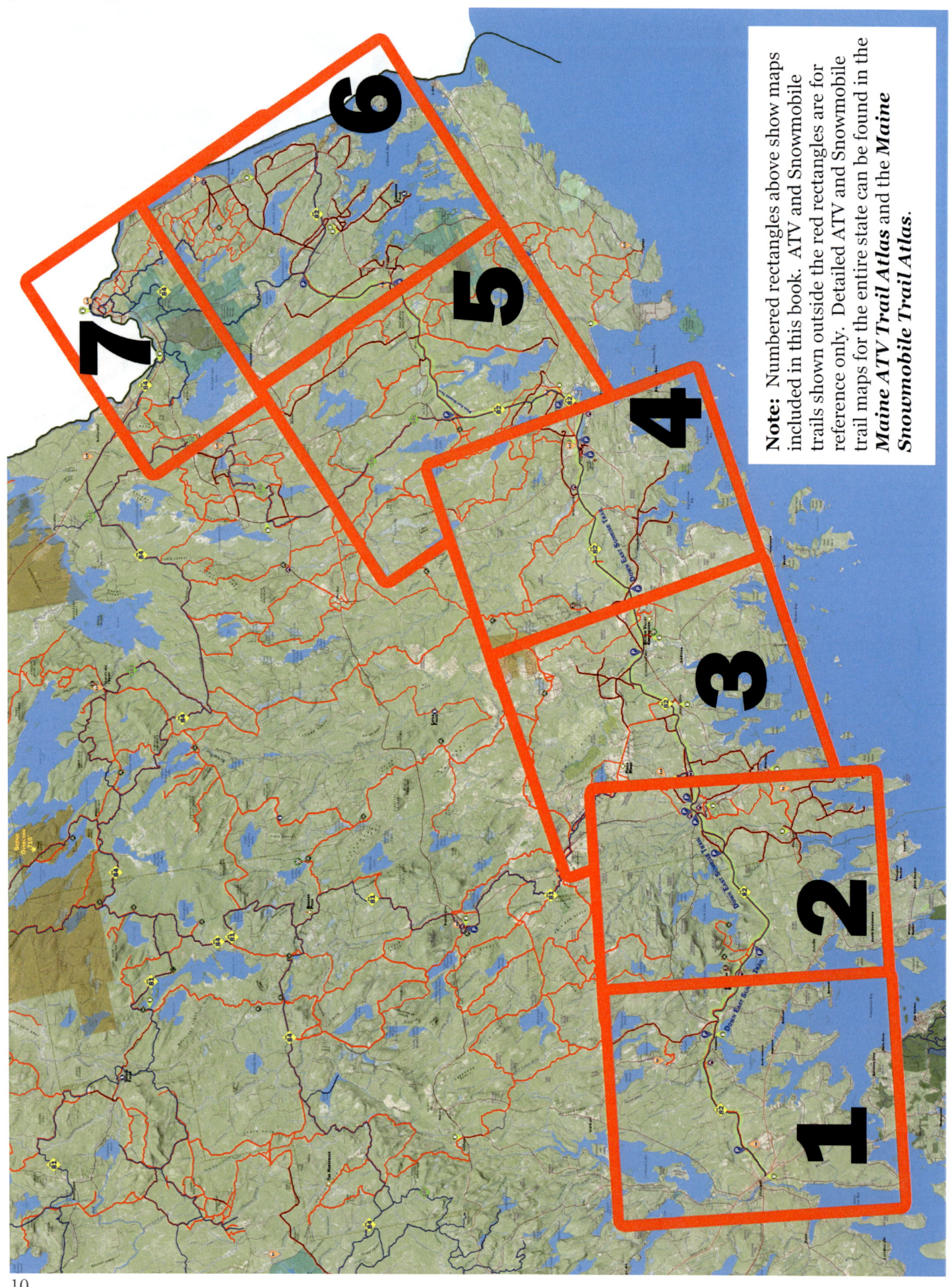

Note: Numbered rectangles above show maps included in this book. ATV and Snowmobile trails shown outside the red rectangles are for reference only. Detailed ATV and Snowmobile trail maps for the entire state can be found in the *Maine ATV Trail Atlas* and the *Maine Snowmobile Trail Atlas.*

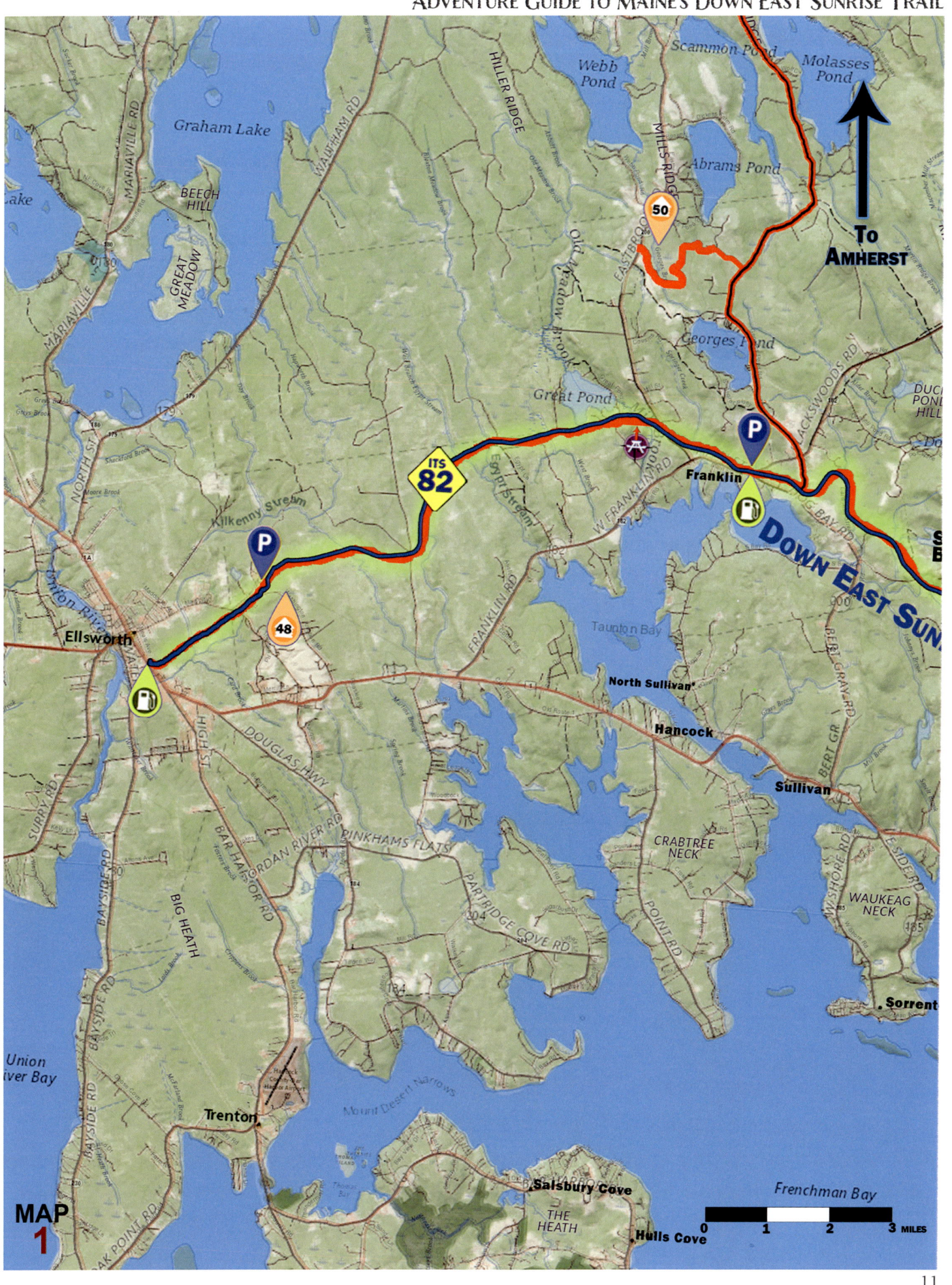

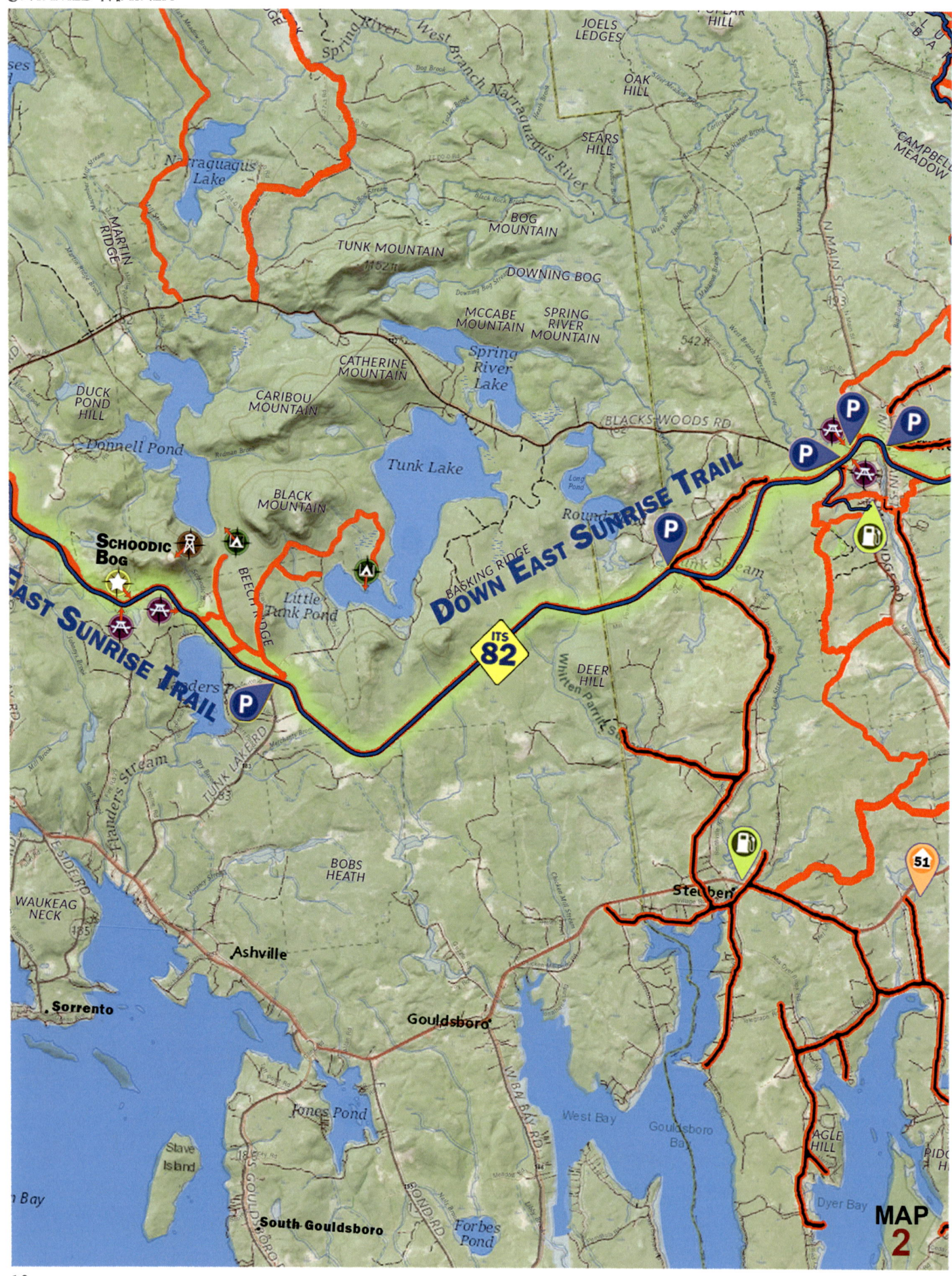

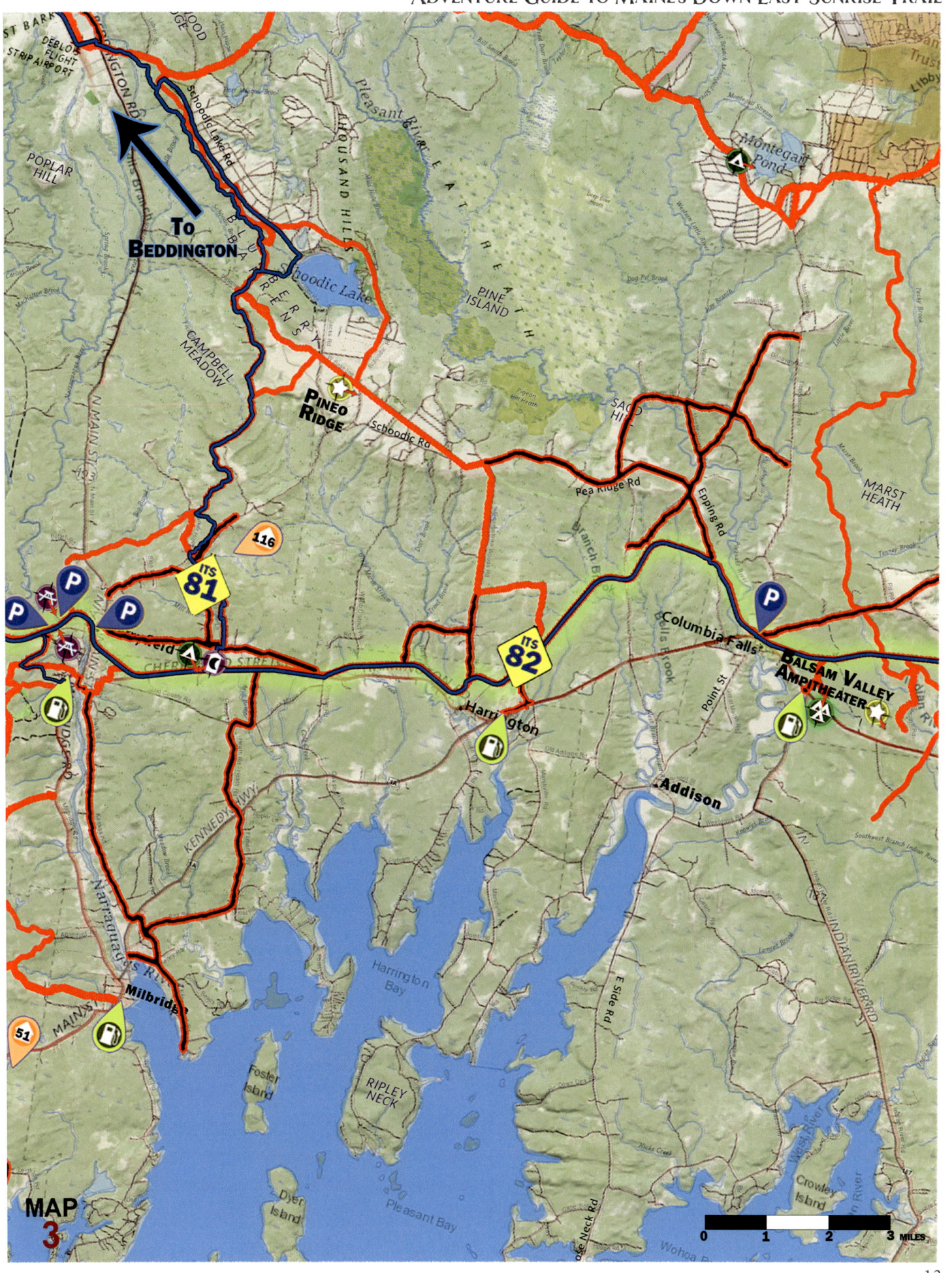

TO
BEDDINGTON

PINEO
RIDGE

116

ITS
81

ITS
82

Columbia Falls

BALSAM VALLEY
AMPITHEATER

Harrington

Addison

Milbridge

51

MAP
3

0   1   2   3 MILES

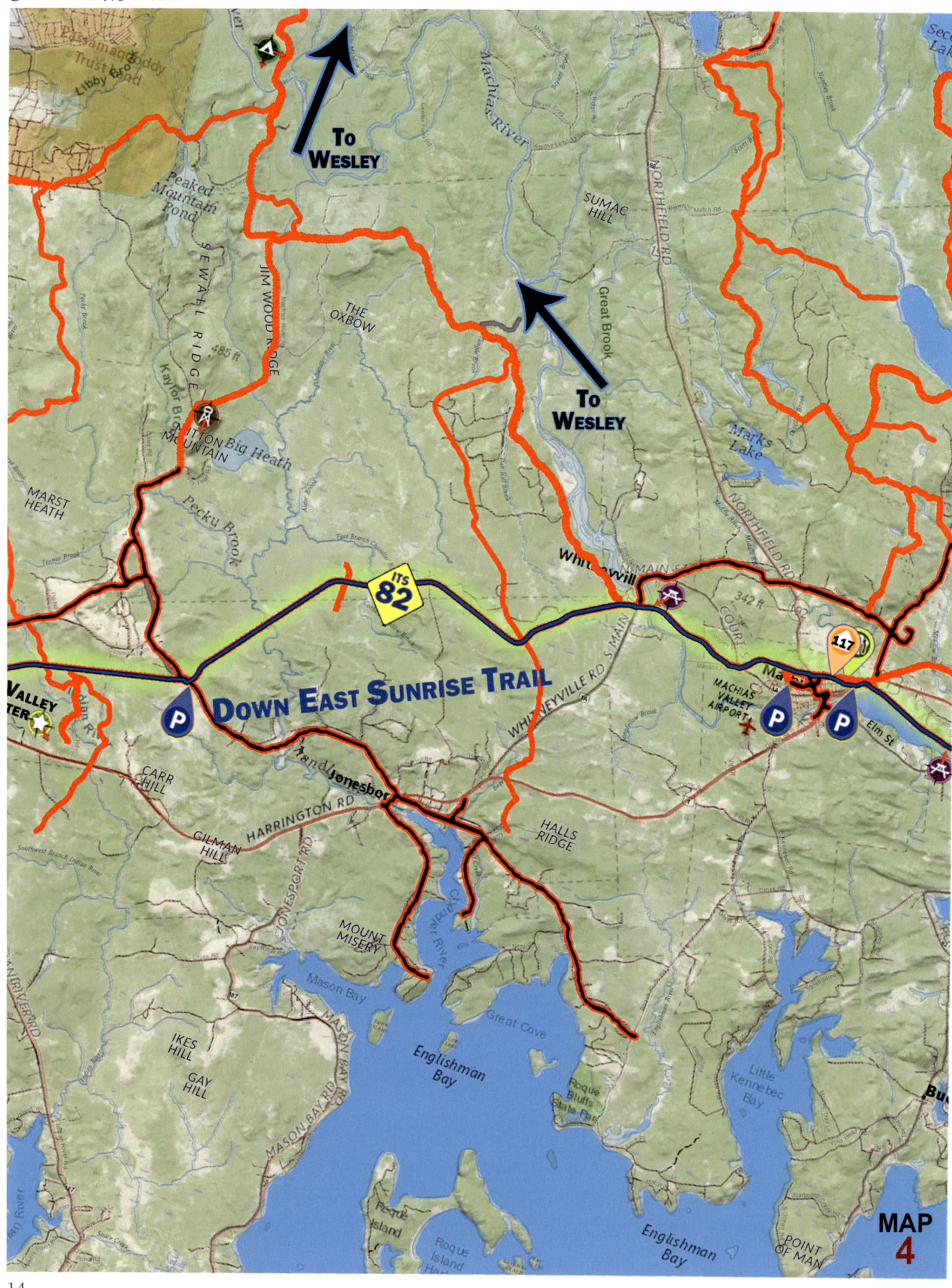

To WESLEY

To WESLEY

THE OXBOW

ITS 82

DOWN EAST SUNRISE TRAIL

MAP 4

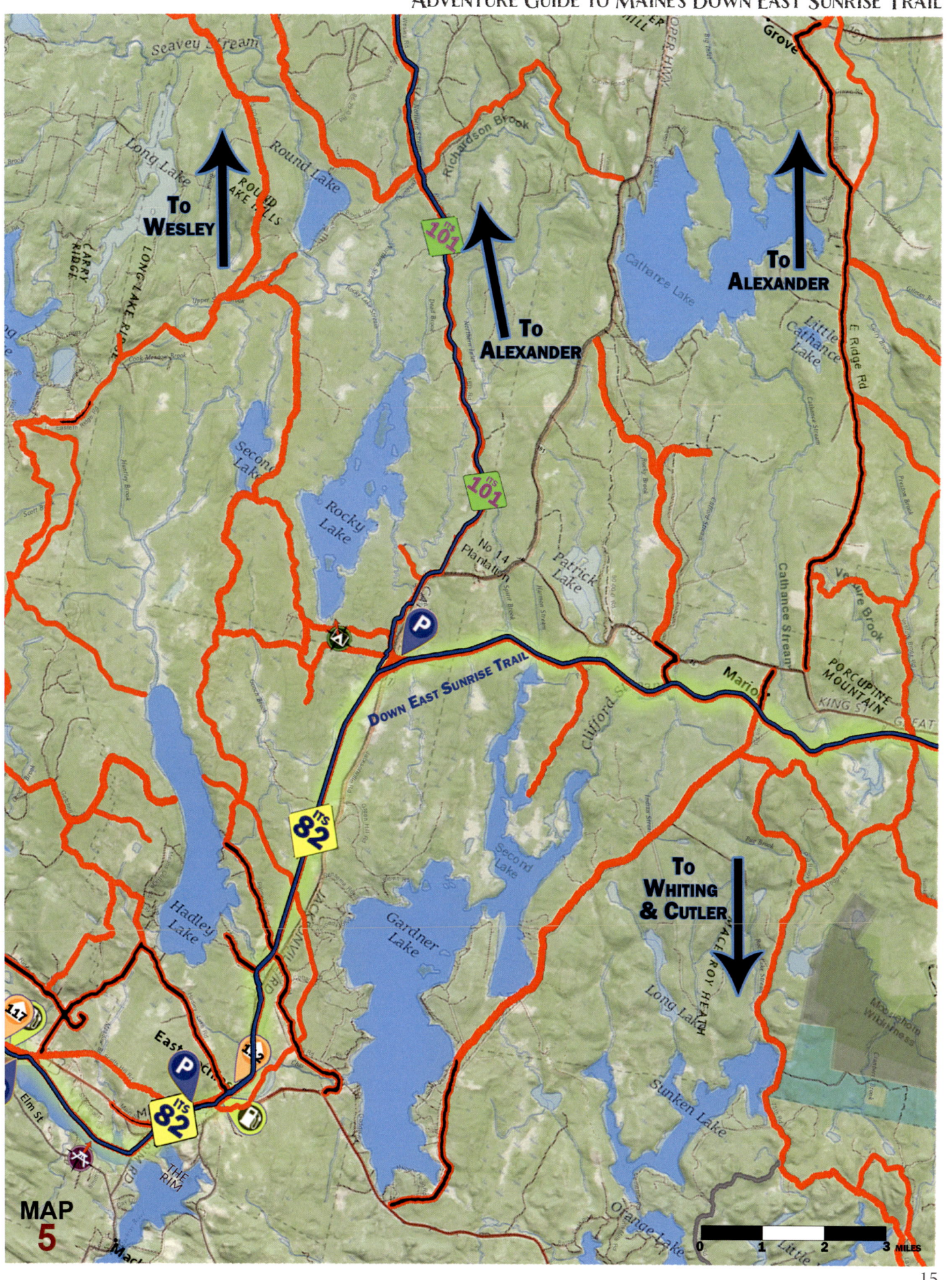

TO
WESLEY

TO
ALEXANDER

TO
ALEXANDER

ITS
101

ITS
101

TO
WHITING
& CUTLER

ITS
82

ITS
82

Down East Sunrise Trail

MAP
5

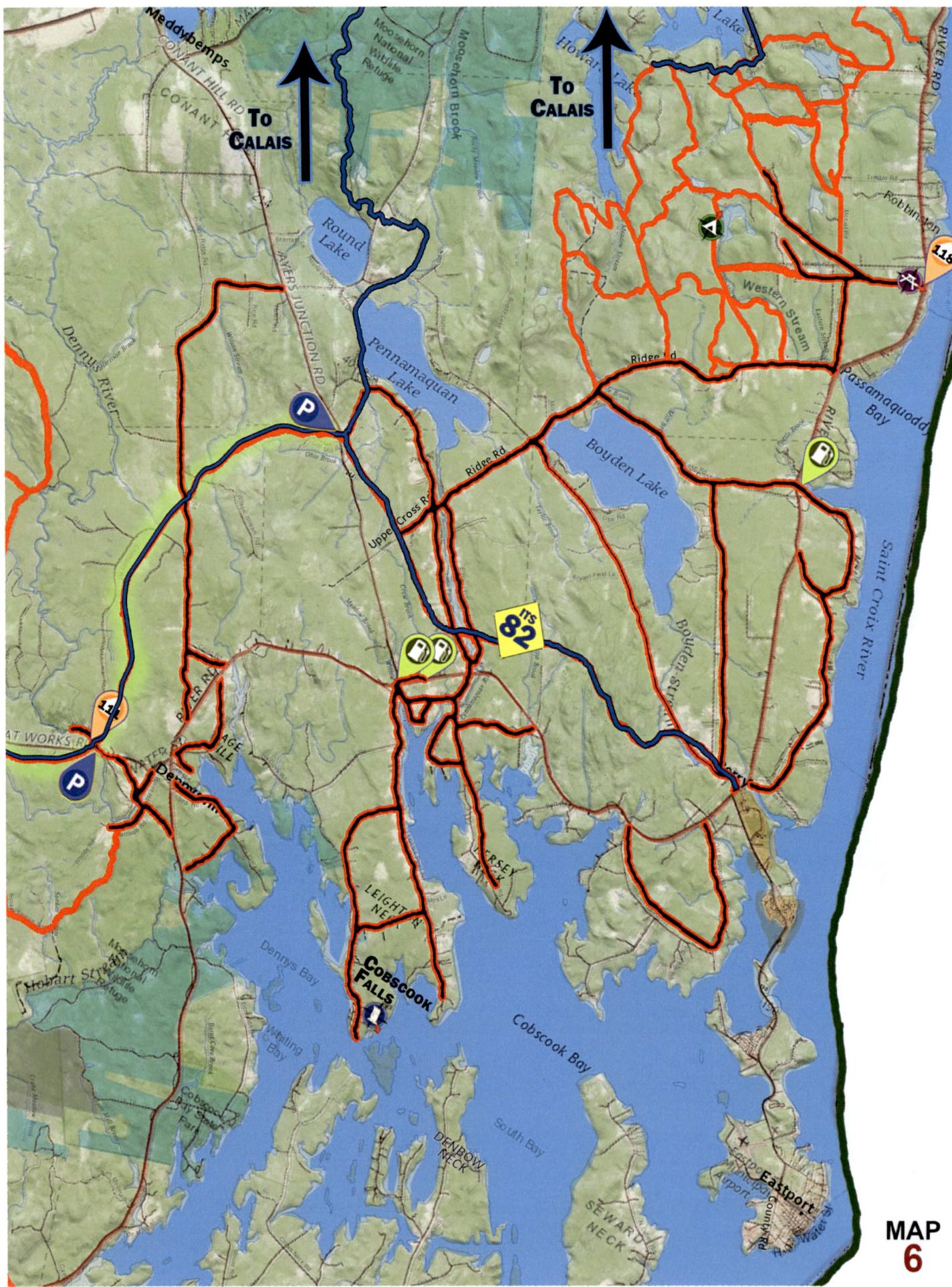

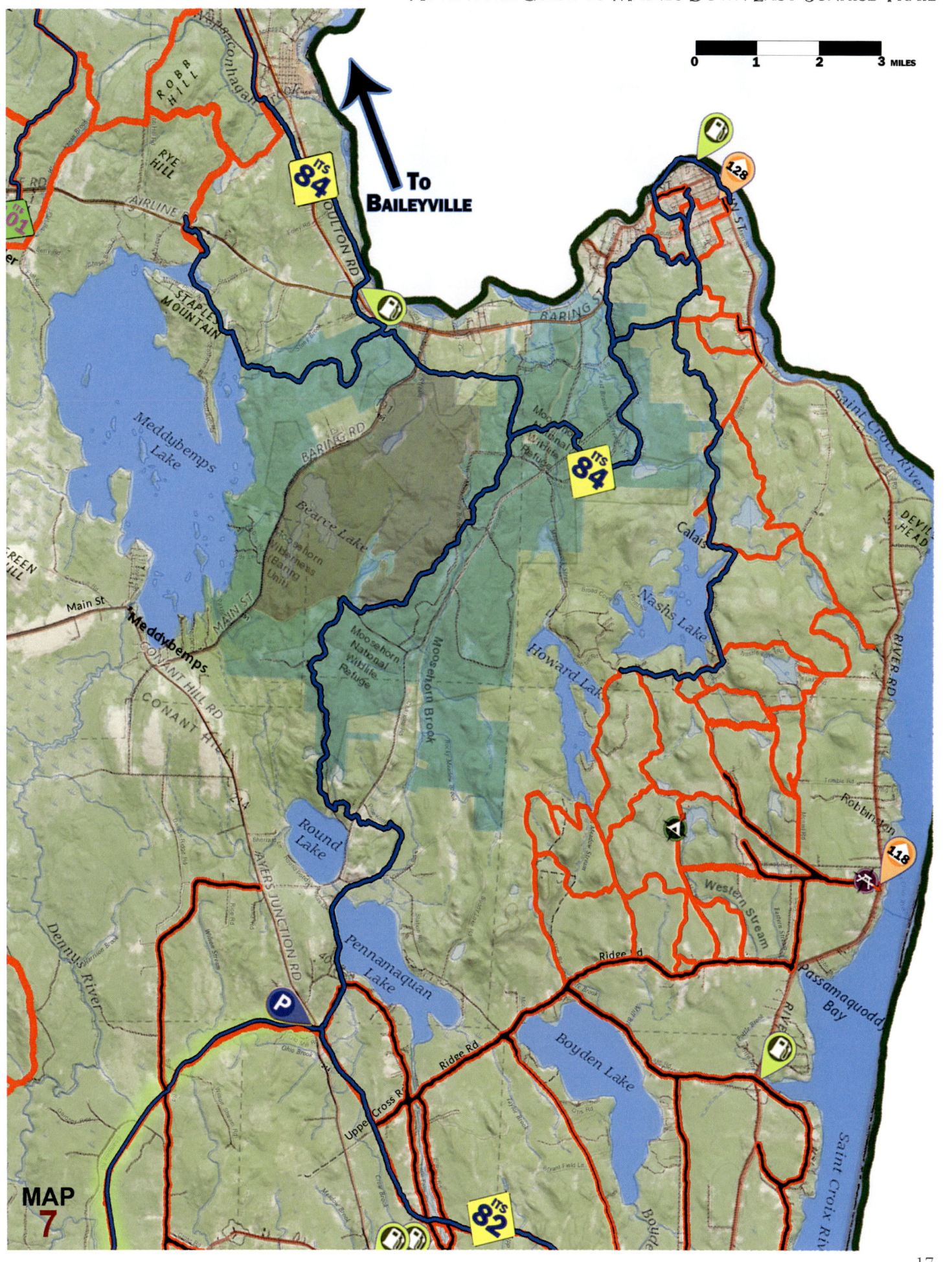

0   1   2   3 MILES

ROBB HILL

RYE HILL

STAPLES MOUNTAIN

ITS 84

To BAILEYVILLE

AIRLINE RD

HOULTON RD

BARING SHO...

Saint Croix River

DEVIL HEAD

Meddybemps Lake

BARING RD

Bearce Lake

Moosehorn Wilderness Baring Unit

ITS 84

Moosehorn National Wildlife Refuge

Calais

Nashs Lake

Howard Lake

GREEN HILL

Main St

Meddybemps

CONANT HILL RD

CONANT HILL

Moosehorn National Wildlife Refuge

Moosehorn Brook

RIVER RD

Robbinston

Round Lake

AYERS JUNCTION RD

118

Dennys River

Pennamaquan Lake

Western Stream

Ridge Rd

Passamaquod... Bay

P

Ridge Rd

Boyden Lake

Upper Cross Rd

Saint Croix River

MAP 7

ITS 82

DEST DIRECTIONS

-0.5 MILE MARKER, ELLSWORTH- FUEL, FOOD, LODGING

Page 23. The Down East Sunrise Trail (DEST) extends to High Street in Ellsworth where many trail-side services are available for ATVs and snowmobiles. There are many other places to eat and stay in the area that are easily accessible if you are walking or biking the trail.

0 MILE MARKER, ELLSWORTH- PICNIC TABLE

44.540417, -68.404371 Official mile marker zero location.

2 MILE MARKER, HANCOCK- PARKING, LODGING, PICNIC TABLES

Washington Junction Trail Head, page 24. There are two very large parking lots at this location to leave your vehicle and trailer. On holiday weekends arrive early because the lots fill up fast. The first parking lot is where Acadia Area ATV'ers clubhouse is located. There used to be an ATV rental service located across the street which is no longer in operation. **Treehouse Getaways** is located just across the road from the second parking lot.

11 MILE MARKER, FRANKLIN- FUEL, FOOD, SUPPLIES, LIMITED PARKING

Franklin Crossing, page 25. **Franklin Trading Post** 207-565-3314. Franklin Trading Post is accessible from the trail. Cross Blackwoods Road in Franklin and look for the trail on your left leading through the woods just a short bit to the back of the parking lot. Gas pumps are open 24/7, the store is open Monday - Saturday, 6am-8pm, and Sunday 8am-7pm, and the restaurant serves food from 6am to 1pm. The store also carries basic supplies like goggles, hand warmers, gloves, etc. The parking lot offers limited parking.

11.5 MILE MARKER, FRANKLIN

Access Route to Trail #500. Trail #500 continues northeast crossing Route 9 and connects to Trail #503 and #510 towards Amherst.

16 ¾ MILE MARKER, FRANKLIN- HIKING TRAILS, PRIMITIVE CAMP SITES, OUTHOUSES

Donnell Pond Public Lands, page 33. Dirt roads that intersect the trail to the north are open to ATVs- Schoodic Beach Road and Black Mountain Road. The dirt roads lead to parking areas where hiking trailheads are located. An outhouse is located near the parking lot at the end of Schoodic Beach Road, and from there it's a half-mile hike to Schoodic Beach on Donnell Pond. Schoodic Beach offers an incredible view of Donnell Pond and Schoodic Mountain, several outhouses, picnic tables, and 5 small campsites, and 2 large group campsites, all with picnic tables and fire rings.

18 MILE MARKER, SULLIVAN- PARKING

Tunk Lake Road, ME 183. Second ATV access route to Donnell Pond Public Lands via Black Mountain Road and Schoodic Beach Road. Trailside parking.

DEST DIRECTIONS

25.5 MILE MARKER, UNIONVILLE- PARKING
Unionville Crossing. Limited parking area.

29 ¼ MILE MARKER, CHERRYFIELD- FOOD
Page 26. North Street Cafe 207-546-7780 Open Wednesday, Thursday, & Sunday 11am - 7pm and Friday & Saturday 11am - 8pm.

29.5 MILE MARKER, CHERRYFIELD- PARKING, PICNIC TABLE
Cable Pool, page 26. Scenic park on the Narraguagus River near a dam, limited parking. One covered picnic table.

30 MILE MARKER, CHERRYFIELD- PARKING
Cherryfield Crossing, page 26. Limited parking area.

30.5 MILE MARKER, CHERRYFIELD- GROCERIES
Willey District Road, page 26. CH Mathews grocery store 207-546-2601, open Monday - Friday 9am - 8pm.

31 MILE MARKER, CHERRYFIELD- DOWNTOWN CHERRYFIELD
Loop trail to Steuben. Trail leaves DEST towards Steuben and loops back to DEST at Mile Marker 29 ¼.

32 MILE MARKER, MILBRIDGE- PRIMITIVE CAMPSITES, OUTHOUSE
Sunrise Campground, accessible by DEST only, free camping. Six primitive campsites are located just off the trail on a first-come, first-served basis. These are simple, cleared sites in the woods with a fire ring.

32.5 MILE MARKER, MILBRIDGE- ATV TRAILS & ITS JUNCTION
ATV Trail 504 & MATS 105, ITS Trail 81. Connector trail for ATVs and snowmobiles to Airline Lodge & Diner 30 miles north for food, fuel, and lodging 207-638-2301 open Monday - Saturday 6am - 6pm and Sunday 7am - 6pm.

36 MILE MARKER, MILBRIDGE- PARKING
Narraguagas High School. Parking is allowed during summer break, holidays, and weekends only. No parking while school is in session.

DEST DIRECTIONS

37 MILE MARKER, HARRINGTON- FOOD
Page 27. **Scovils Millside Dining** 207-483-6544 open Tuesday - Sunday, 11am - 7pm.

37.5 MILE MARKER, HARRINGTON- FOOD, FUEL, CAMPING
Page 27, ATV Trail 514 Junction. **Harrington Irving** 207-483-4694, open 24/7 & **Subway** 207-483-2420, open daily 10am - 8pm, accessible 1 ½ miles via trail and access route on Harrington Road. **Sunset Point Campground** 207-483-4412 accessible via trail then 3 miles down Marshville Road ATV access route to Sunset Point Road. Scovils Millside Dining 207-483-6544 located just ¼ mile south from the trail via North Street to Route 1 access route. Open Tuesday - Sunday 11am - 7pm.

43 MILE MARKER, COLUMBIA FALLS- FOOD, PARKING
Tibbetstown Road Crossing, page 28. Limited parking area. Follow access route from Centerville Road to Tibbetstown Road to Main Street to reach **Columbia Falls General** 207-483-8092 serving local food and ice cream.

44 MILE MARKER, COLUMBIA FALLS- FUEL, FOOD, CAMPING
Page 28. Trail accessible services ¾ mile from DEST. **Cottonwood Camping & RV Park** 207-598-8497 adventure campground. Cottonwood offers ATV/dirt bike and horse-friendly trail accessible camping. The campground offers full hookup RV camping, tent camping, and rents a teepee, tents, and a treehouse. **Elmers Country Store** 207-483-2100 offering food and fuel, open Monday - Saturday 6am - 8pm and Sunday 7am - 7pm. **Pleasant River Drive-In** 207-483-2900 serves seafood, burgers, ice cream, sandwiches and more, open Monday - Saturday 11:30am - 7pm and Sunday 12pm - 7pm. **Wild Blueberry Land** 207-483-2583 bakery & ice cream, open Friday, Saturday, and Sunday 9am - 2pm.

47 MILE MARKER, JONESBORO- JUNCTION, FOOD
Jonesboro Station Road. Trail 516 to Holmes Falls and ATV access route to Jonesboro. **Downeaster Restaurant & Tap Room** *(formerly Swamp Yankee BBQ)* 207-434-2068, head southeast at the junction for 4 miles.

54 MILE MARKER, WHITNEYVILLE- PARKING
Whitneyville Crossing. Huge parking lot on the DEST off Middle Street in Whitneyville, has a stationary dirt ramp for loading ATVs and snowmobiles into trucks.

DEST DIRECTIONS

58.5 MILE MARKER, MACHIAS- FUEL, FOOD, LODGING, OUTDOOR GEAR, PARKING

Machias, page 29, Hiking Trails page 32. Machias Chamber of Commerce: http://machiaschamber.org

FUEL:

Irving Oil, open 24/7 for food and fuel 207-255-4228

FOOD: There are many places accessible just off the trail via access routes. Some of the closest to the trail are listed below.

Subway 207-255-4900 open 9am - 10pm daily

Helen's Takeout/Delivery 207-255-8423 open Tuesday, Thursday, and Friday 10:30am - 7pm, Wednesday 10:30am - 2pm, Saturday 7am - 7pm, and Sunday 8am - 2pm

River's Edge Drive In 207-259-6258 open Monday - Saturday 11am - 7pm and Sunday 12pm - 7pm

Jo's World Famous Schnitzel Wagon 207-200-3001 open Monday - Saturday 11am - 7pm

The Bluebird Ranch Family Restaurant 207-255-3351 open Monday - Thursday 11am - 7pm, Friday 7am - 8pm, and Saturday and Sunday 7am - 7pm

Hing Garden 207-255-8881 open Sunday - Thursday 11am - 9pm and Friday & Saturday 11am - 10pm

Thirsty Moose Cafe 207-255-6100 open Monday - Saturday 11am - 9pm

Dunkin' Donuts 207-255-6218 open daily 5am - 8pm

Pat's Pizza 207-255-8111 open Monday - Thursday 11am - 7pm, Friday 11am - 8pm, and Saturday 11am - 7pm

LODGING:

Machias River Inn 207-255-4861

Inn at Schoppee Farm 207-540-5504

OUTDOOR GEAR:

Sunrise Canoe & Kayak 207-255-3375 open Monday - Friday 9am - 2pm

62 MILE MARKER, EAST MACHIAS- FUEL, FOOD, LODGING, PARKING

Page 30. Lodging & food at **The Riverside Inn & Restaurant** 207- 255-4134, fuel & food at **Archibald's One Stop** 207-255-3827 **last fuel stop on the DEST heading east** and **The Talbot House Inn** 207-259-1103 or 207-217-2620

70 MILE MARKER, EAST MACHIAS- JUNCTION

East Machias/Berry TWP. Junction to MATS 101 (ATV) and ITS 101 (snowmobile) towards Maine Public Reserved Land- Rocky Lake Unit (approximately 2 miles), and Wesley/Grand Lake Stream area. Rocky Lake Unit has ATV, snowmobile, and hiking trails, 3 trailside primitive campsites, and outhouses.

DEST DIRECTIONS

78.5 MILE MARKER, DENNYSVILLE- JUNCTION

Dodge Road. Junction to ITS 522. Take 522 north 27 miles for food and fuel at McLoed's Store in Alexander, where you can continue on to Woodland and Princeton. Take 522 south for 14 miles for food and fuel at Whiting Store in Whiting, where you can continue on 11 miles further to reach A2Z Variety for food and fuel in Cutler.

80 MILE MARKER, DENNYSVILLE- CAMPING

Page 31. Robinson's Cottages 207-726-9546 seasonal trail accessible cottages on the Dennys River.

80.5 MILE MARKER, DENNYSVILLE- CLUBHOUSE, FOOD, SUPPLIES, PARKING

Page 31. Dennysville Snowmobile & ATV Club 207-263-6306 Clubhouse is open 24/7 although there isn't always someone there. A Pepsi vending machine and picnic tables are outside the building and a snack vending machine and tables are inside the building. The inside vending machine has a variety of items like snacks, ibuprofen, and trail maps. Both vending machines are cash only. The club hosts breakfasts open to everyone, check their Facebook page for more information.

87 MILE MARKER, PEMBROKE- PARKING, EAST END OF DEST

Ayers Junction. Huge parking lot at the easternmost end of the DEST. There is a DEST extension that begins directly across the road that leads to Perry, Robbinston, and Calais.

ELLSWORTH

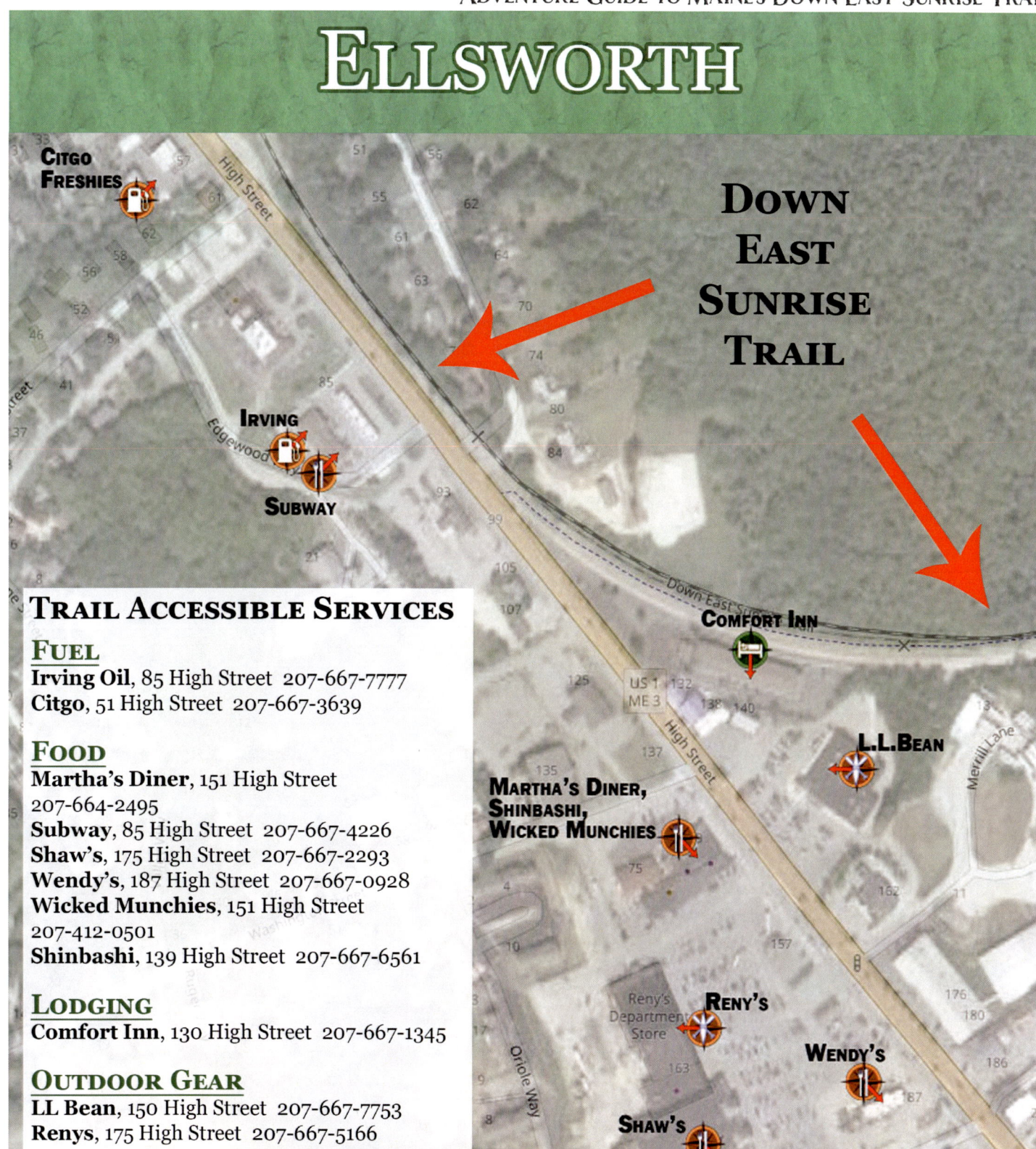

DOWN EAST SUNRISE TRAIL

TRAIL ACCESSIBLE SERVICES

FUEL
Irving Oil, 85 High Street 207-667-7777
Citgo, 51 High Street 207-667-3639

FOOD
Martha's Diner, 151 High Street
207-664-2495
Subway, 85 High Street 207-667-4226
Shaw's, 175 High Street 207-667-2293
Wendy's, 187 High Street 207-667-0928
Wicked Munchies, 151 High Street
207-412-0501
Shinbashi, 139 High Street 207-667-6561

LODGING
Comfort Inn, 130 High Street 207-667-1345

OUTDOOR GEAR
LL Bean, 150 High Street 207-667-7753
Renys, 175 High Street 207-667-5166

NEARBY ESSENTIAL SERVICES

ELLSWORTH CHAMBER OF COMMERCE
163 High Street 207-667-5584
https://www.ellsworthchamber.org/

OUTDOOR GEAR
Cadillac Mountain Sports, 32 High Street 207-288-4532
Olympia Sports, 225 High Street #8 207-667-7532

ATV & SNOWMOBILE SALES/SERVICE
Friend & Friend, 227 State Street 207-667-4688
D's Motorsports, 739 Bucksport Road 207-249-4077

WASHINGTON JUNCTION

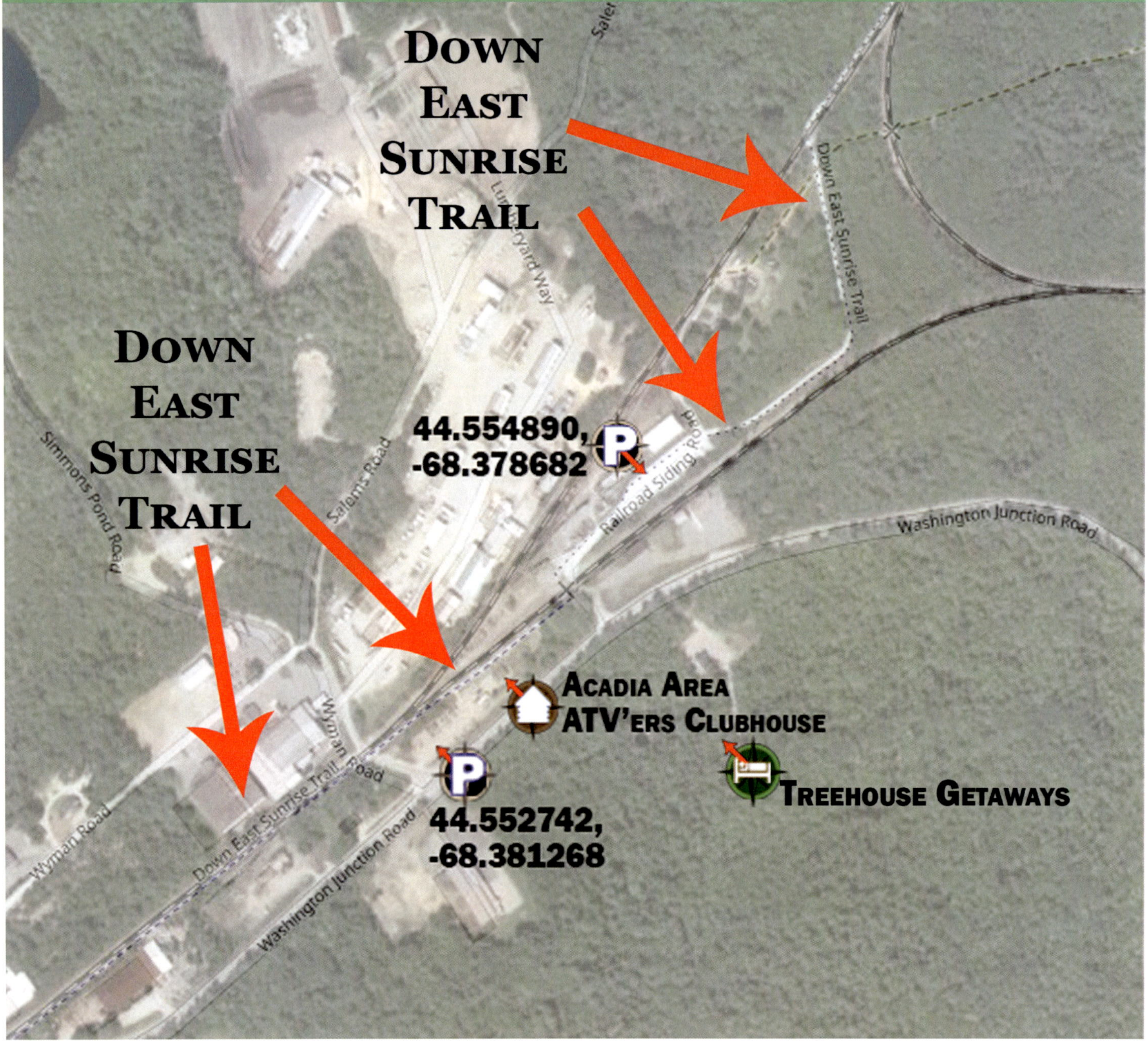

DOWN EAST SUNRISE TRAIL

DOWN EAST SUNRISE TRAIL

44.554890, -68.378682 🅿

🅿 44.552742, -68.381268

🏠 ACADIA AREA ATV'ERS CLUBHOUSE

🛏 TREEHOUSE GETAWAYS

TRAIL ACCESSIBLE SERVICES

LODGING
Treehouse Getaways, Washington Junction Road. Single rental, sleeps 8, 4 beds, must reserve ahead of time online at https://tinyurl.com/y5pjxnu2

ATV CLUB
Acadia Area ATV'ers, Washington Junction Road. 207-963-2506

FRANKLIN CROSSING

44.588359,
-68.231777

FRANKLIN TRADING POST

P

Winter Road

Down East Sunrise Trail

Railroad Siding

44.588524,
-68.223275

Down East Sunrise Trail

ME 182

Franklin

Hog Bay Road

11 MILE MARKER- FUEL, FOOD, SUPPLIES, LIMITED PARKING

Franklin Crossing. Franklin Trading Post 207-565-3314. Franklin Trading Post is accessible from the trail. Cross Blackwoods Road in Franklin and look for the trail on your left leading through the woods just a short bit to the back of the parking lot. Gas pumps are open 24/7, the store is open Monday - Saturday, 6am-8pm, and Sunday 8am-7pm, and the restaurant serves food from 6am to 1pm. The store also carries basic supplies like goggles, hand warmers, gloves, etc. The parking lot behind their paved lot offers limited parking.

The DEST parking lot is accessible by taking Route 182 & Route 200 into Franklin and turning onto Winter Road.

ATV Trail #514 Junction

No shortage of beautiful scenery along the trail

CHERRYFIELD

44.608066,
-67.937506

44.608761,
-67.926101

Cherryfield Dam

CH MATTHEWS
GROCERY

NORTH STREET CAFE

44.605034, -67.937527

TRAIL ACCESSIBLE SERVICES

FOOD

North Street Cafe, 109 North Street
207-546-7780
CH Mathews AG, 141 Main Street
207-546-2601

Fantastic trail conditions

Junction Marker

HARRINGTON

DOWN EAST SUNRISE TRAIL

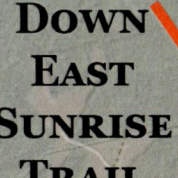

TRAIL ACCESSIBLE SERVICES

FUEL
Irving, 1141 Main Street 207-483-9628

FOOD
Scovils Millside Dining, 1276 Main Street
207-483-6544
Subway, 1141 Main Street 207-483-2420

LODGING
Sunset Point Campground, 24 Sunset Point
Road 207-483-4412

·········· **Dirt Road Access Route**
·········· **Paved Road Access Route**

Straight trails for miles!

Columbia Falls

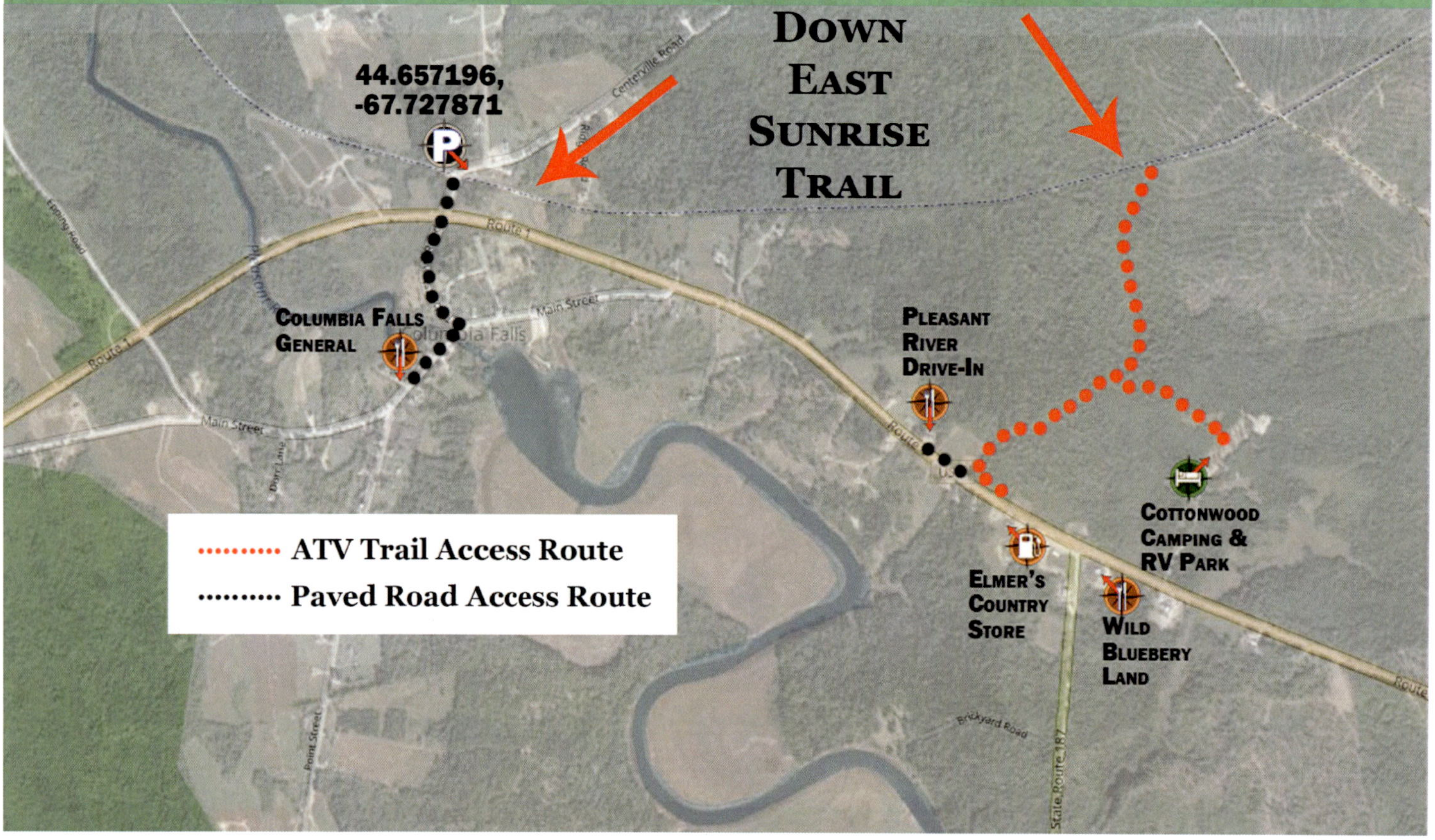

44.657196,
-67.727871

Down East Sunrise Trail

.... ATV Trail Access Route
.... Paved Road Access Route

Columbia Falls General

Pleasant River Drive-In

Elmer's Country Store

Wild Bluebery Land

Cottonwood Camping & RV Park

Trail Accessible Services

Fuel
Elmer's Country Store, 1039 US-1
207-483-2100

Food
Columbia Falls General, 150 Main Street
207-483-8092
Pleasant River Drive-In, 990 Harrington
Road 207-483-2900
Wild Blueberry Land, 1067 US-1
207-483-2583

Lodging
Cottonwood Camping & RV Park, 1140
US-1 207-598-8497

Cherryfield Dam and Cable Pool

Scenic view from the trail

Panoramic view in East Machias

MACHIAS

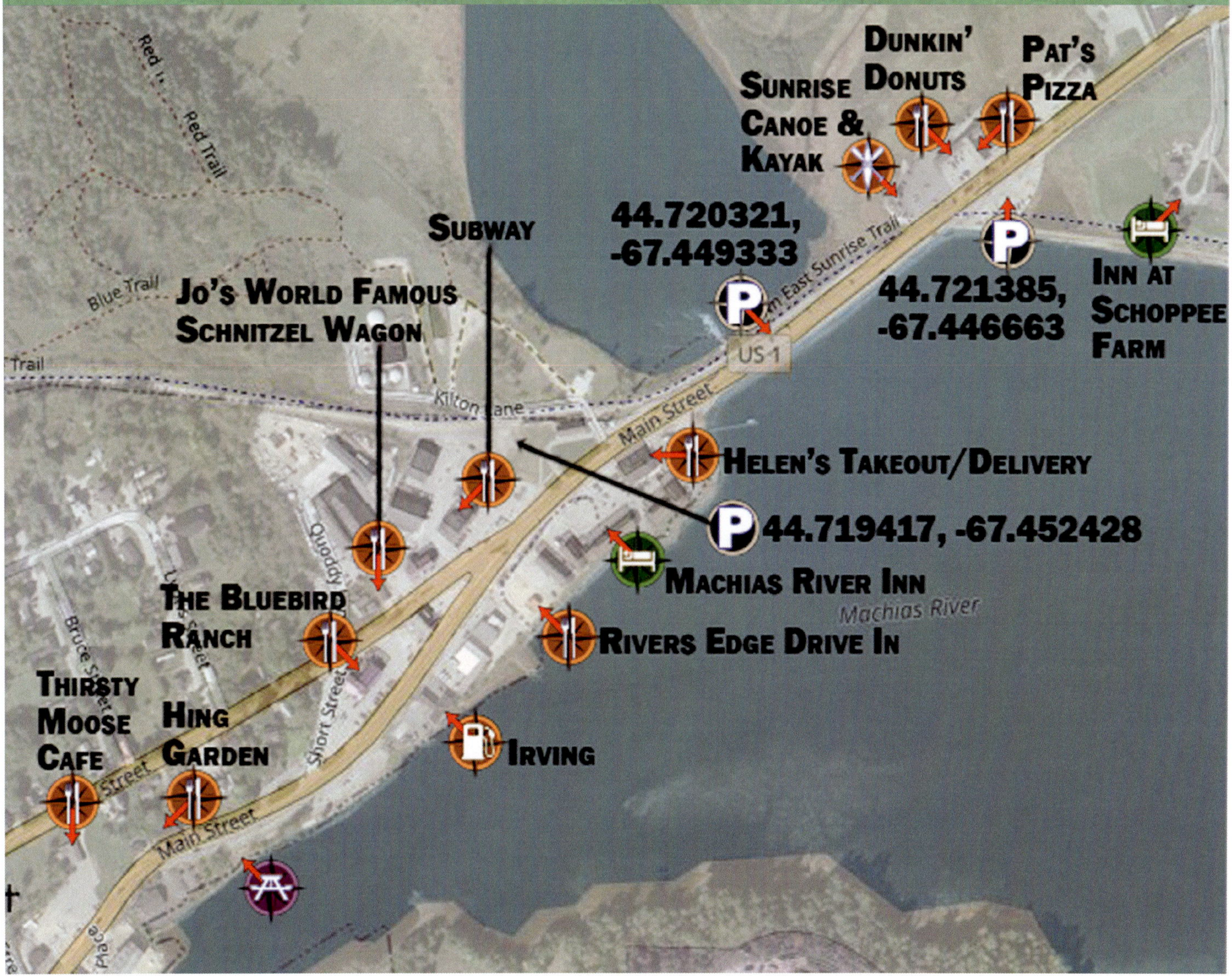

DUNKIN' DONUTS

PAT'S PIZZA

SUNRISE CANOE & KAYAK

SUBWAY

44.720321, -67.449333

44.721385, -67.446663

INN AT SCHOPPEE FARM

JO'S WORLD FAMOUS SCHNITZEL WAGON

HELEN'S TAKEOUT/DELIVERY

44.719417, -67.452428

MACHIAS RIVER INN

THE BLUEBIRD RANCH

RIVERS EDGE DRIVE IN

THIRSTY MOOSE CAFE

HING GARDEN

IRVING

TRAIL ACCESSIBLE SERVICES

FUEL
Irving 207-255-4228

FOOD
Subway 207-255-4900
Helen's Takeout 207-255-8423
River's Edge Drive In 207-259-6258
Jo's World Famous Schnitzel Wagon
207-200-3001
The Bluebird Ranch Family Restaurant
207-255-3351
Hing Garden 207-255-8881
Thirsty Moose Cafe 207-255-6100
Dunkin' Donuts 207-255-6218
Pat's Pizza 207-255-8111

LODGING
Machias River Inn 207-255-4861
Inn at Schoppee Farm 207-540-5504

OUTDOOR GEAR
Sunrise Canoe & Kayak 207-255-3375

EAST MACHIAS

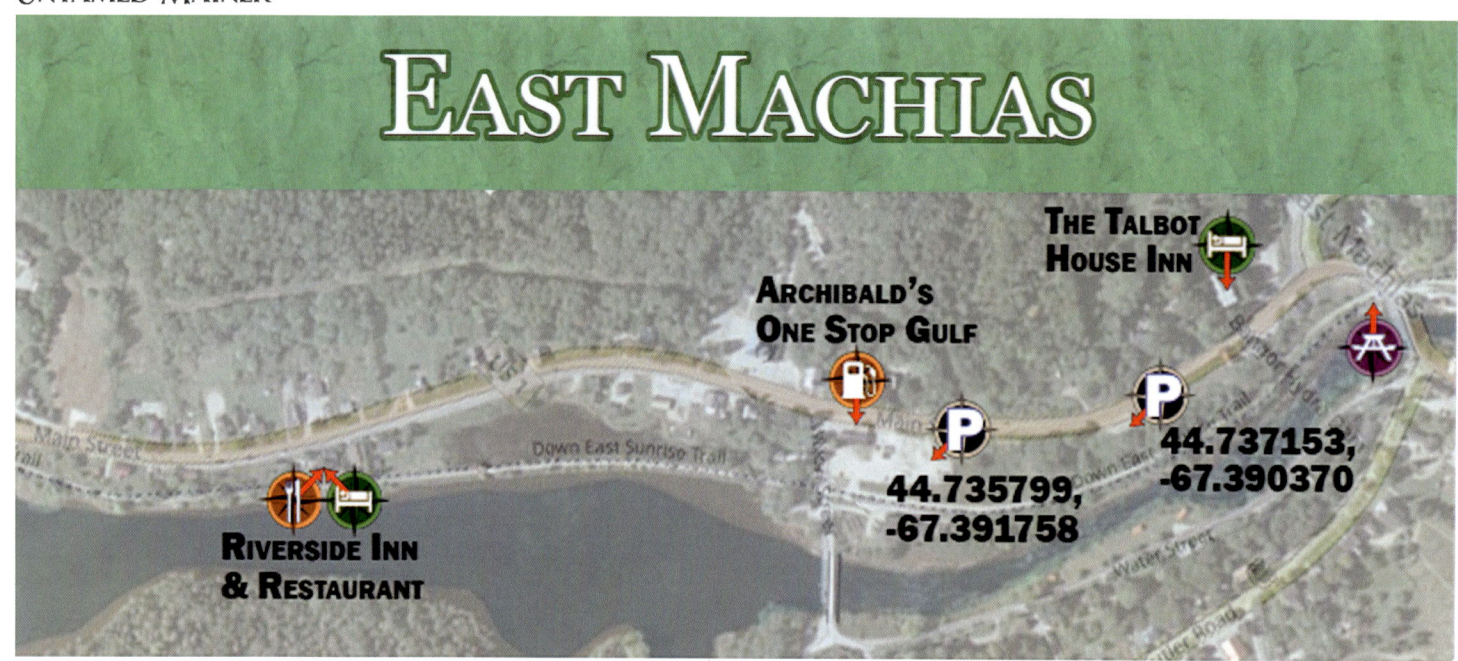

THE TALBOT HOUSE INN

ARCHIBALD'S ONE STOP GULF

44.737153, -67.390370

44.735799, -67.391758

RIVERSIDE INN & RESTAURANT

TRAIL ACCESSIBLE SERVICES

FUEL
Archibald's One Stop-Gulf, 564 Main Street
207-255-3827

FOOD
Riverside Inn & Restaurant, 622 Main Street
207-255-4134

LODGING
Riverside Inn & Restaurant, 622 Main Street
207-255-4134
The Talbot House Inn, 509 Main Street
207-259-1103

DENNYSVILLE

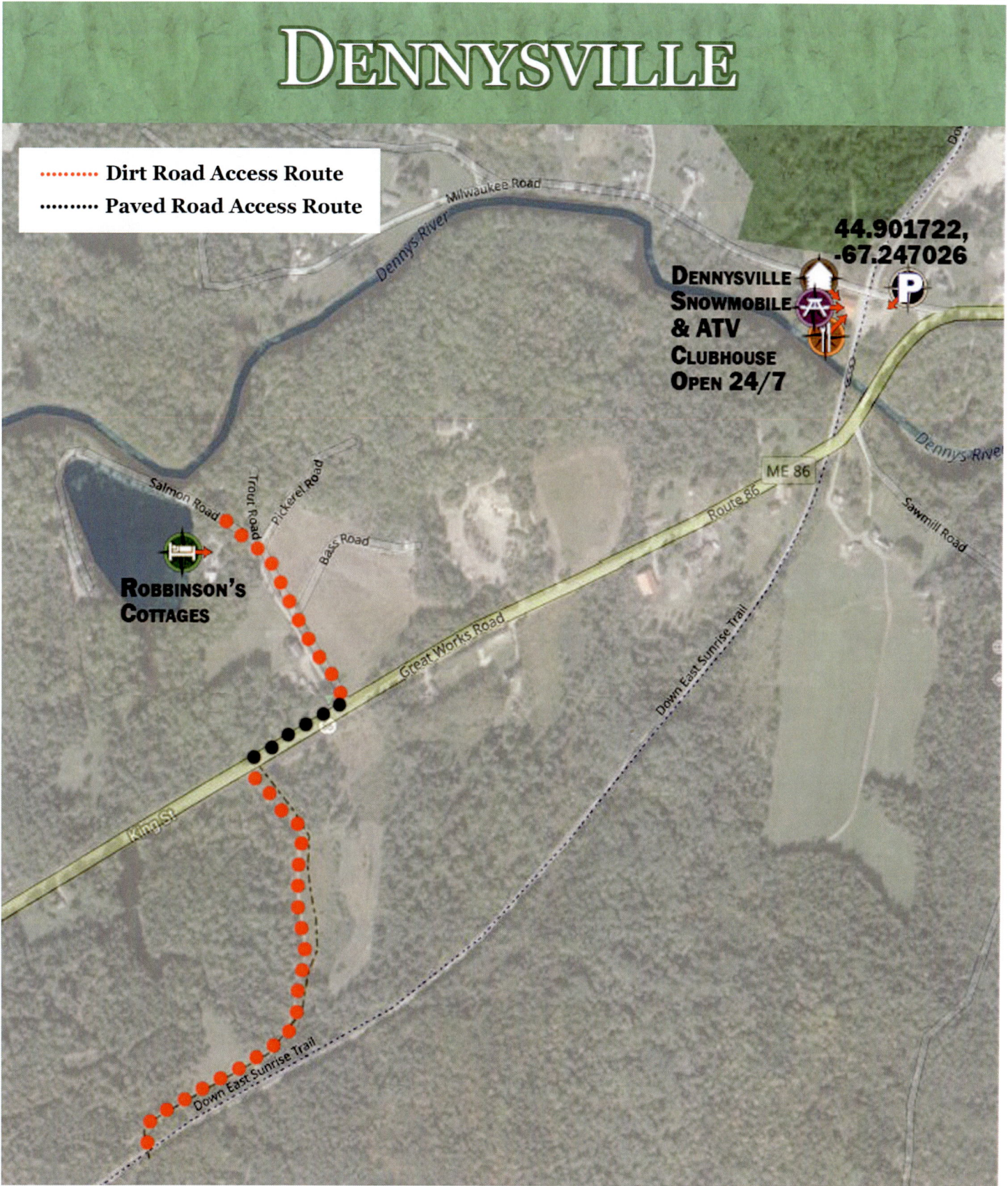

Dirt Road Access Route
Paved Road Access Route

44.901722, -67.247026

DENNYSVILLE SNOWMOBILE & ATV CLUBHOUSE OPEN 24/7

ROBBINSON'S COTTAGES

TRAIL ACCESSIBLE SERVICES

FOOD
Dennysville Snowmobile & ATV Clubhouse, King Street
207-263-6306
Occasionally has breakfasts, vending machines on site, bring cash.

LODGING
Robinson's Cottages, 253 King Street
207-726-9546

MACHIAS HIKING TRAILS

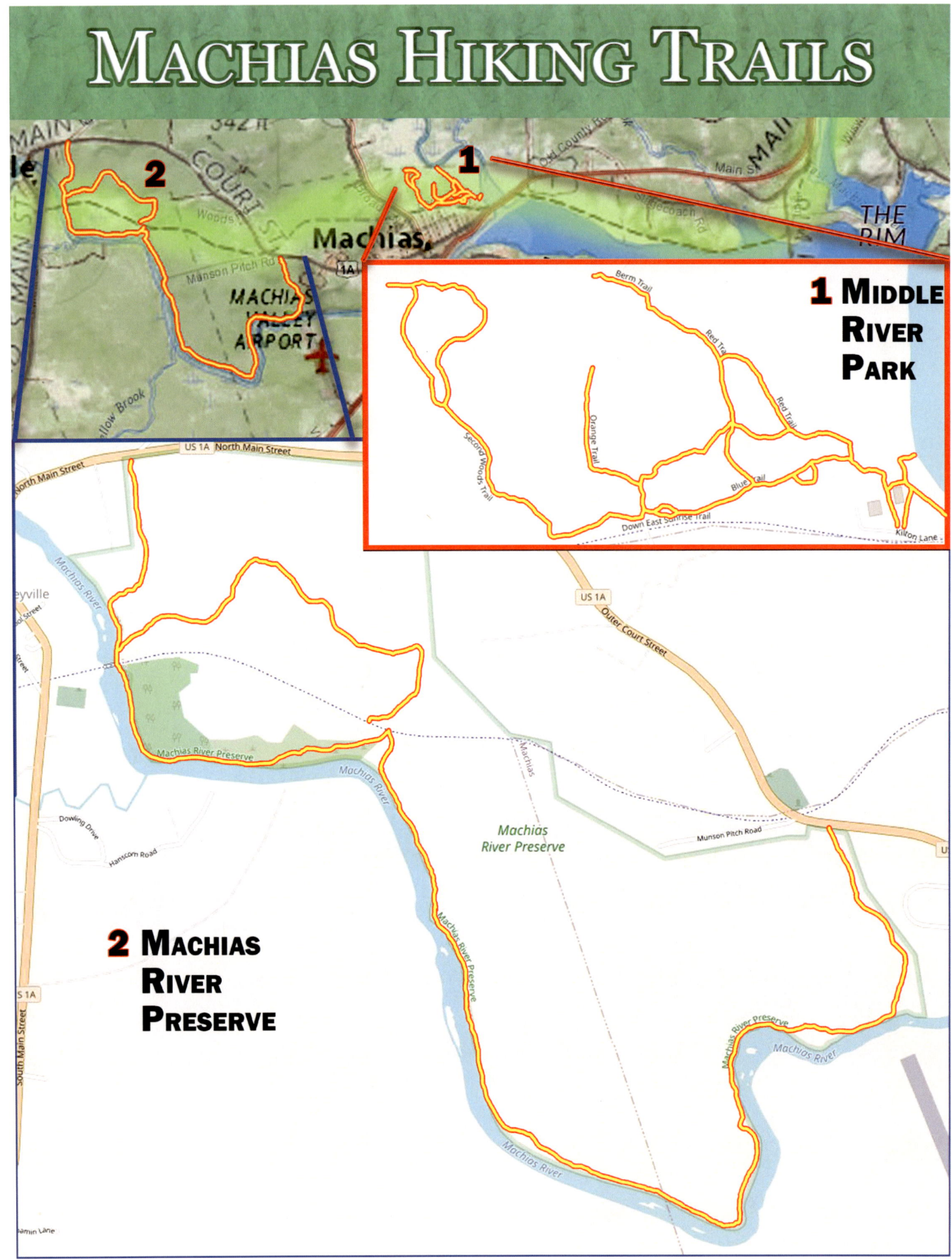

2

1

1 MIDDLE RIVER PARK

Berm Trail

Red Trail

Red Trail

Orange Trail

Second Woods Trail

Blue Trail

Down East Sunrise Trail

Kilton Lane

US 1A North Main Street

North Main Street

US 1A

Outer Court Street

Machias River

Machias River Preserve

Machias River Preserve

Machias River

Machias River Preserve

Machias River

Dowling Drive

Hanscom Road

Munson Pitch Road

2 MACHIAS RIVER PRESERVE

Donnell Pond PRL & Franklin Area Hiking Trails

PARKING LOCATIONS

Parking lots can fill up very fast on weekends and holidays. Washington Junction's 2 parking lots are the most popular and tend to fill up the quickest because it's the largest parking area and the closest for most visitors. All GPS parking lot coordinates below are large enough for trailer parking unless noted otherwise.

WASHINGTON JUNCTION, MILE MARKER 1.5
Washington Junction Road, Hancock
Lot #1 GPS: 44.552742, -68.381268
Lot #2 GPS: 44.554890, -68.378682
PAGE 24

There are two very large parking lots at Washington Junction to leave vehicles and trailers. The first parking lot is where Acadia Area ATV'ers clubhouse is located.

FRANKLIN CROSSING, MILE MARKER 11
Blackswoods Road, Route 182, Franklin
Lot #1 GPS: 44.588359, -68.231777
Lot #2 GPS: 44.588524, -68.223275
PAGE 25

There are two decent-sized parking lots at this location. The first lot is trailside and accessible by taking Route 182 to Winter Road. After crossing the DEST (watch for traffic) the parking lot will be on your left. The second parking lot is at Franklin Trading Post. The lot is the dirt pad you will see to the right of the building just beyond the paved parking. The trail to the DEST is just beyond the parking lot.

TUNK LAKE ROAD, MILE MARKER 18
Tunk Lake Road, Route 183, Sullivan
Trailer Lot GPS: 44.548894, -68.111485
Non-Trailer Lot GPS, Schoodic Beach: 44.573954, -68.130151
Non-Trailer Lot GPS, Big Chief Trail: 44.577449, -68.104753
PAGE 34

There is only one parking lot in this location big enough for vehicles and trailers. The Schoodic Beach parking area can hold about 20 vehicles and tends to fill up fast. The Big Chief Trail parking area is located off Black Mountain Road and can hold 2-3 vehicles.

UNIONVILLE CROSSING, MILE MARKER 25.5
Unionville Road, Steuben
Lot GPS: 44.578440, -67.990302
This is a smaller parking lot located along the trail and roadside but it is large enough for several trailers.

PARKING LOCATIONS

NORTH STREET CAFE, MILE MARKER 29 ¼
109 North Street, Cherryfield
Lot GPS: 44.604980, -67.937693
This is a smaller trailside parking lot located next to the cafe. The lot can hold a handful of trailers.

CABLE POOL, MILE MARKER 29 ½
Cable Pool Road, Cherryfield
Lot GPS: 44.608565, -67.938021
This is a smaller parking lot located in Cable Pool Park. The lot can hold a handful of trailers.

CHERRYFIELD CROSSING, MILE MARKER 30
Route 193, Cherryfield
Lot GPS: 44.608747, -67.926014
This is an interesting-shaped parking lot that could potentially hold a good number of trailered vehicles depending on how others park. It is a reasonable-sized dirt pad that continues on as a dirt road loop-around to the DEST.

CH MATHEWS AG, MILE MARKER 30 ½
Route 193 & Willey district Road, Cherryfield
Lot GPS: 44.607508, -67.926014
This parking lot is smaller but can hold under 20 vehicles with trailers. The parking lot is located across the street from CH Mathews AG.

NARRAGUAGUS HIGH SCHOOL, MILE MARKER 36
1611 Main Street, Harrington
Lot GPS: 44.619720, -67.841317
This is a decent sized parking lot that is only available during the summer and weekends when school is not in session.

TIBBETSTOWN ROAD CROSSING, MILE MARKER 43
Centerville Road & Tibbetstown Road, Columbia Falls
Lot GPS: 44.657202, -67.727938
This is another smaller parking lot located on both sides of the DEST that can hold a handful of trailers.

STATION ROAD JUNCTION, MILE MARKER 47
Station Road, Jonesboro
Lot GPS: 44.670059, -67.646449
This is another smaller parking lot located alongside of the DEST that can hold a handful of trailers.

PARKING LOCATIONS

WHITNEYVILLE CROSSING, MILE MARKER 55
10 Middle Street, Whitneyville
Lot GPS: 44.719545, -67.522963

This is a large parking lot that can hold a lot of trailers. This is the only parking lot along the DEST that has a stationary dirt ramp for loading ATVs and snowmobiles into trucks.

MACHIAS, MILE MARKER 58 ½
Route 1, Machias
Trailer Lot GPS, Kilton Lane: 44.719449, -67.452422
Non-Trailer Lot GPS, Bridge: 44.720249, -67.449389
Trailer Lot GPS, Across from Dunkin': 44.721361, -67.446642
PAGE 29

The town of Machias has several lots available for DEST parking. The first lot off Kilton Lane is next to the Machias Chamber of Commerce. The lot can hold a good number of trailers. Another parking location for the DEST is on the bridge that spans the river, although vehicles with trailers are not allowed to park on the bridge. There is a fair amount of parking available on the bridge, although keep in mind local vendors often set up shop on the bridge and can take up several of the spaces. The last parking location is over the bridge across from Dunkin'. This is a fair-sized lot that can hold a good number of trailers depending on how people park. This lot sits right next to the DEST.

EAST MACHIAS, MILE MARKER 62
Route 1, East Machias
Lot GPS, Archibald's One Stop: 44.735799, -67.391758
Lot GPS, Main Street: 44.737153, -67.390370
PAGE 30

The parking lot at Archibald's is much larger and easier for trailers. The second parking lot just up the road on Main Street is much smaller but can hold a few trailers but is better for trailerless vehicles.

EAST MACHIAS, MILE MARKER 70
Cathance Road, Route 191, East Machias
Lot GPS: 44.834646, -67.420268

This is another small trailside parking lot that can hold a few trailers.

DENNYSVILLE, MILE MARKER 80 ½
Milwaukee Road, Dennysville
Lot GPS: 44.901723, -67.247050

This parking lot is located at the Dennysville Snowmobile & ATV clubhouse. The lot is large and can fit a good number of trailers.

PARKING LOCATIONS

AYERS JUNCTION, MILE MARKER 87
Ayers Junction Road, Route 214, Pembroke
Lot GPS: 44.986171, -67.236453

This is a large parking lot and is the east end of the DEST. The parking lot can hold a very large number of trailers.

Nice loading ramp in the Whitneyville Crossing parking lot

Dennysville Clubhouse and parking area

Washington Junction parking lot #1

RESTROOM LOCATIONS

ELLSWORTH
Irving Oil, 85 High Street
Citgo, 51 High Street
Martha's Diner, 151 High Street
Subway, 85 High Street
Shaw's, 175 High Street
Wendy's, 187 High Street
Shinbashi, 139 High Street
LL Bean, 150 High Street
Renys, 175 High Street

HANCOCK
Washington Junction, 2 Railroad Siding

FRANKLIN
Franklin Trading Post, 33 Blackwood Road

CHERRYFIELD
North Street Cafe, 109 North Street
CH Matthews AG, 141 Main Street
Sunrise Campground (May-November only), Mile Marker 32

HARRINGTON
Irving, 1141 Main Street
Scovils Millside Dining, 1276 Main Street
Subway, 1141 Main Street

COLUMBIA FALLS
Elmer's Country Store, 1039 US-1

MACHIAS
Machias Bay Chamber of Commerce, 2 Kilton Lane
Irving, 8 Main Street
Subway, 1 Court Street Unit 5
The Bluebird Ranch Family Restaurant, 78 Main St
Hing Garden, 46 Main Street
Thirsty Moose Cafe, 36 Main Street
Dunkin' Donuts, 300 East Main Street
Pat's Pizza, 168 Main Street

EAST MACHIAS
Archibald's One Stop-Gulf, 564 Main Street
Riverside Inn & Restaurant, 622 Main Street

DENNYSVILLE
Dennysville Snowmobile & ATV Club, 24 Milwaukee Road

Some parts of the old rail bed are still intact

ATV & SNOWMOBILE TRAIL ACCESS ROUTES

THE DOWN EAST SUNRISE TRAIL IS MATS (MAINE ALL-TERRAIN TRAIL SYSTEM) 206 FOR ATVs AND ITS (INTERCONNECTED TRAIL SYSTEM) 81 FOR SNOWMOBILES

11.5 MILE MARKER- FRANKLIN
ATV: Trail #500 north to Eastbrook & Spectacle Pond

28 MILE MARKER- STEUBEN
ATV: Access Road (Unionville Road) south to Steuben (fuel) and Milbridge (fuel)

31 MILE MARKER- CHERRYFIELD
ATV: Trail #514 south to Steuben and Milbridge

32.5 MILE MARKER- MILBRIDGE
ATV: Trail #504 north, MATS 105 north to Schoodic Lake, Deblois, Beddington, ATV Trail #515, 30 miles to Airline Lodge and Diner and 60 miles to Jack's Snack Shack
ATV & Snowmobile: ITS 81 north to Airline Lodge and Diner

37.5 MILE MARKER- HARRINGTON
ATV: Trail #514 west, in 17 miles the trail intersects with ATV Trail #504 north

54.5 MILE MARKER- WHITNEYVILLE
ATV: Trail #516 to Holmes Falls, Grand Lake Stream for food & fuel or to Airline Lodge and Diner

58.75 MILE MARKER- MACHIAS
ATV: Trail #100 to Hadley Lake and ATV Trail #519

70.5 MILE MARKER- EAST MACHIAS/BERRY TWP
ATV & Snowmobile: ITS 101 to Rocky Lake Public Land for camping, Wesley for food & Fuel, and Grand Lake Stream

78.9 MILE MARKER- DENNYSVILLE
ATV & Snowmobile: Trail #522 north: towards Cathance Lake, 27 miles to fuel heading towards Alexander, Woodland, and Princeton, south: 14 miles south to Whiting Store for food and fuel, 25 miles to A2Z Variety in Cutler for food and fuel.

LODGING LOCATIONS

Please note: not all lodging options are available or open year-round. Call ahead or check online for availability.

ELLSWORTH
Comfort Inn, 130 High Street, 207-667-1345

HANCOCK
Treehouse Getaways, Washington Junction Road, reservations online only

FRANKLIN
Donnell Pond Public Lands, primitive campsites, first come, first served basis

MILBRIDGE
Sunrise Campground (May-November only), Mile Marker 32, first come, first served basis

HARRINGTON
Sunset Point Campground, Marshville Road to Sunset Point Road, 207-483-4412

COLUMBIA FALLS
Cottonwood Camping & RV Park, 207-598-8497

MACHIAS
Machias River Inn, 207-255-4861
Inn at Schoppee Farm, 207-540-5504

EAST MACHIAS
Riverside Inn & Restaurant, 622 Main Street
The Talbot House Inn, 207-259-1103

DENNYSVILLE
Robinson's Cottages, 207-726-9546

East Machias

DEST PHOTOS

DEST PHOTOS

Schoodic Mountain

www.ingramcontent.com/pod-product-compliance
Lightning Source LLC
Chambersburg PA
CBRC090829120626
46547CB00008B/632